Words

POETRY BY:

Kenzie D.

Palmetto Publishing Group, LLC
Charleston, SC

Copyright ©2016 Kenzie D.

ISBN-13: 978-1-944313-20-3
ISBN-10: 1-944313-20-6

Acknowledgements

I would like to accredit this book to my late best friend. To the one who always pushed me to be better and to believe in myself. To the girl who was like a sister to me since diapers. To the one I shared crazy adventures with and unmeasurable hours of laughter. Thank you for always reading my pieces and encouraging me to be better than I thought I could be. Ever since we were in middle school you always pushed me to publish my work, I would have never had the confidence to do this without you. I only wish you were here to see it.

Fly high, Candice Jo.

What a glorious adventure it is to
love another more than the
world knew possible.
-Kenzie D.

Since losing you I've been scared of the fact that
surrounds me, now ever present in my mind.
We are never promised tomorrow to spend together.
We are never promised another adventure,
another memory.

And frankly, that shakes me to my core.
-Kenzie D.

I write to be someone else,
I write to express the things inside of me,
I write to get out the things I could never say.
-Kenzie D.

She loved the color pink and words that rhymed.
She loved the way ink looked on paper and
the smell of fresh cut grass.
She loved to go on wild adventures and
she yearned for people long gone.
But her concern laid so heavily in others
assumptions of her journey
that she went her whole life without
sharing the phenomenon that
made her soul a masterpiece, her life a gallery.
-Kenzie D.

You spent every day acting as if you were disappointed with the outcome of your life but what did you expect? You fell in love with a soul that would break her own back to please you, if only she knew how.
-Kenzie D.

She was drunk on the
peaks of the mountains
and oblivious to the
depth of the valleys.
-Kenzie D.

When you open yourself up to the world,
When you let things hurt you,
that is when you truly find yourself.
Where the blood and tears meet you will
find the parts of you that have been missing.
-Kenzie D.

In that moment of blinding clarity it all became clear.
She had been so focused on being who others wanted
that she lost all want for who she was.

-Kenzie D.

He was sunshine
on a cold day.
The way the sunlight
touched her face.
He was the rain that
danced upon her window.
The breeze that
pushed at her back.
He was the grass
that tickled her feet.
He was summertime.
-Kenzie D.

Kenzie D.

When love becomes tedious
and life becomes labored,
it is time to leave material
things behind you and
become one with nature.
Clarity will surround you.
-Kenzie D.

My heart beats from my chest and
my thoughts are unsure.
Fear holds me at the edge terrified of the fall.
Never have I done anything as dangerous as loving you.
-Kenzie D.

The scent of old worn paper,
The feeling of words that thousands have read,
The stains on the pages from where the
words evoked emotion,
The coffee ring on the cover,
The torn and ripped binding.
In a world so entranced by technology
isn't it magical to hold a
piece of paperback history?
-Kenzie D.

He wasn't made to be a part of the
war breaking out around him,
for he had yet to conquer the
war within himself.
-Kenzie D.

Depths of emotion plague my very existence.
I hate how much I loved you, how weak I
allowed myself to become in the wake of
your hurricane.
Broken bones and scarred skin,
I loved you still.
-Kenzie D.

It is nothing but natural to fly, my darling.

-Kenzie D.

It is quite tiring when your mind travels to the
ends of the earth time and time again
only to be met with the same regrets of yesterday.
-Kenzie D.

Let's take a road trip,

start an adventure without ever leaving home.

As the wine slips through my veins and

awakens the parts of me that I have forced to hibernate.

Show me the dreams that you

have never shared with another,

the uncharted territory of your soul.

-Kenzie D.

As she lay awake before the sun had
even risen she silently begged for sleep
to overcome her, to quiet her restless mind.
She burrowed deeper into her cocoon of
blankets trying to stop the shivering,
trying to warm her soul.
-Kenzie D.

My mind wanders to the places I'll never go
with the people I'll never meet
and it feels like home.
-Kenzie D.

Oh, but to be free.

To be unshackled from those who pull you down.

To soar above the others in the way you were designed.

To break from the norms and give no thought to society.

Oh, but to be free.

-Kenzie D.

What a blessing it is to live a simple life
in a complicated world.
-Kenzie D.

Life is a constant battle between
loving people and losing people.
-Kenzie D.

She could never thank him enough for loving her.

Truly and relentlessly, without waiver.

For gluing her broken pieces back together.

For loving the flaws that others could never see past.

For not laughing at her fear of storms.

For eating every bite even when she burnt dinner.

For laughing at her stupid jokes and

listening to every endless story.

For wiping tears and holding her hand through it all.

-Kenzie D.

You cannot be both the
cop and the criminal.
-Kenzie D.

And there she stood,
beautifully and innocently confused
by the cruelty that surrounded her.
A mere child,
she had seen more than most and
yet she still couldn't grasp
the anger that consumed them.
-Kenzie D.

The chorus of crickets from the trees
wrapped them in a beautifully poetic tune,
as if the forest was playing a
lullaby for only them to hear.
-Kenzie D.

Raindrops stream from her eyes as her mind is
clouded by the thoughts of what used to be.
-Kenzie D.

Oh, what a mess it is inside my head.
Where the flowers grow wild and
caged animals roam free.
A place where all things are possible and the
most absurd of ideas seem the most sane.
-Kenzie D.

Exhaustion overcame her and forced her eyes
to void the images before them.
She fell into a realm where memories and
imagination danced, creating a glorious song.
There she found peace.
-Kenzie D.

When your heart is so full it feels as if it may burst,
when tingles run up your spine
at the sound of their name,
when silence becomes comfortable,
when colors become more vibrant and
the world seems more beautiful.
That is happiness.
That is love.
-Kenzie D.

She became so broken that she didn't believe it was
possible to be loved again,
but despite it all, he loved every single shattered piece
until she finally felt whole.
-Kenzie D.

When your skin has
been burnt and
your heart charred,
rise from the ashes.
-Kenzie D.

When the waves kiss your feet and the
breeze hugs you tight,
know that I am nearby. Never have
I left you,
never have I strayed. Know that
I am the glimmer of
hope that says you're never alone.
-Kenzie D.

Wine is poetry set aflame as it
dances through your veins.
-Kenzie D.

Very faintly she remembered the life before him.
In a nightmare where she lay shattered and broken,
where she wanted for everything and bled for everyone,
in a valley she never thought she could climb from.

And then she met him.
-Kenzie D.

Can you hear it?
The peace and quiet calling to us,
the mountains begging us to let them ease our souls.
-Kenzie D.

The hands of the clock ticked ever so
slowly by, hypnotizing her mind.
She daydreamed of the open road that beckoned to her,
knowing full well that she would never answer the call.
But what a deliciously irresponsible thing
it would be to run away.
-Kenzie D.

Her heart was stuck in the void that lies between
carrying on and conforming.
-Kenzie D.

Celebrate those who raise you up.
Those who support you unrelentingly and
bring a shimmer of laughter to often dull days.
-Kenzie D.

Kenzie D.

It was as if the crowds parted to present him,
as if the universe spun in
such a way that it led to serendipity.
Her heart gained motion again at the sight of him.
His eyes held a magic she quit believing in lifetimes ago.
-Kenzie D.

There are still nights when I forget you won't
be there to answer my call.
-Kenzie D.

She often wonders what lies
beyond the horizon.
She likes to think it is a
paradise full of endless wonder
and effortless peace. A
paradise so filled with overwhelming love
that hate wouldn't be recognized.
-Kenzie D.

So many adventures we had yet to embark on,
so many sights yet to be seen.
A thousand miles we should have traveled,
a thousand hours enriched with laughter.
So many sleepless nights I can
almost hear your voice and
every damn time I wish it had
been me instead of you.
-Kenzie D.

Such a soft soul in an otherwise
overwhelmingly rigid world.
-Kenzie D.

As he nuzzled his head into her lap,
she stroked his fur and sighed.
She saw in his eyes a loyalty that
no human could ever replicate.
-Kenzie D.

She lay scattered and tethered all at once.
Her heart clung to him so tightly that it's a
wonder they both didn't suffocate.
Bound by a love she wanted to believe in,
crushed by his wondering eyes.
She feared that she would allow him to tear
her down in the act of building himself up,
forever self-destructive.
-Kenzie D.

Her thoughts were full of wildflowers
that she couldn't gather into bouquets.
-Kenzie D.

She loved the way the keys
slid under her fingers,
permanently pressing all the words
she could never say onto paper.
Something she could rip, crumple and
throw away before anyone had the
chance to misunderstand her.
-Kenzie D.

His laughter is a song I could listen to all day,
his eyes a poem I could never put into words.
-Kenzie D.

What a glorious disaster it is when we find
the one who sets our soul ablaze,
the one who makes the rest of our
life seem dull in the wake of their flames.
While the embers float through the air like fireworks
around you and happiness dances in their eyes,
the world reduces to ash.
-Kenzie D.

I regret every day I wasted before I met you.
Every day that I spent thinking of giving up.
-Kenzie D.

When the thunder shakes the windows and
the lightening engulfs the room,
I search frantically for your hand
among the sheets that intertwine us.
It's a childish fear, but regardless of
how needy and pitiful I sound,
you always pull me close and
hold me until morning light,
so effortlessly slaying the fears that
threaten to rear their ugly heads.
-Kenzie D.

What a wonderful thing it is when one
chooses to understand rather than judge.
-Kenzie D.

I hold those that I love close to my heart,

I cherish every memory,

and photograph every moment I can.

For years from now these will be the times

we laugh about as we sit on Grandpa's front porch and

watch our own muddy children running through the

same field we found ourselves in decades before.

-Kenzie D.

I want the quirky, awkward love
that no one else understands.
-Kenzie D.

An unmade bed,
the smell of coffee at dawn,
she stretches and smiles as
she looks around her at the
beautifully simplistic life she
had created for herself.
-Kenzie D.

Am I a believer?
Oh, I am a believer of many things.
I believe in happily ever after,
I believe in wishing upon shooting stars,
I believe that you leave a piece of your soul in
every single person you have ever loved,
I believe ink on paper cures a broken heart,
and I believe true love is the
most tangible form of magic.
Yes, darling, I am a believer.
-Kenzie D.

She had a heart of gold,
but he was merely a tin man
not sure how to love again.
-Kenzie D.

For so long I thought of you
as my tomorrow but now,
after it all, I don't even think of
you fondly as my yesterday.
-Kenzie D.

As the raindrops slid down her window
she couldn't help but smile as she was
reminded of all the tears she would no longer cry,
the clouded frame of mind long gone.
The day he left the sun showed its glowing face again,
illuminating her new found freedom.
-Kenzie D.

The ink was fresh,
her heart raw.
-Kenzie D.

She was hiding in the shadows
all the while silently screaming to be noticed.
The fear of rejection kept her plastered
to the wall but the need to be loved
kept her internally conflicted,
forever battling herself.
-Kenzie D.

I tried to fit into his life like an elephant
through the eye of a needle.
It was truly laughable at best.
-Kenzie D.

She has a poetic mind.
Where bad and good interlace beautifully,
making the perfect rhythm for a song.
Her heart dances freely with each cord and
feels every single beat in its core,
soothing her soul amongst the waves of the world.
-Kenzie D.

When the words flow through my mind,
I can only hope to catch them as they fly by.
-Kenzie D.

The day slipped through her hands
while she tried to focus,
as if she had attempted to
hold the beach in her palms.
It wasn't until dusk fell
that she realized how
little time she had spent
being thankful for
all the blessings that
kept her busy.
-Kenzie D.

Although she was American born,
her heart spoke every language.
-Kenzie D.

I drove out to the lake we used to
frequent and stood overlooking all the
glorious creations before me.
Then, overwhelmed by the
serenity that confused my muddled mind,
I screamed your name.
The single echo that mocked me
was nearly as frightening as the thought
of my life without you.
-Kenzie D.

You made me feel alive again.
Like a ripple in an otherwise stagnant pond.
-Kenzie D.

She wrapped his sweater tighter
around her and breathed in his scent,
hoping it would warm the lonely chill
that racked her bones.
What a pitiful thing it is to be in love,
finding loneliness in the mere moments of separation.
-Kenzie D.

Those with hopeful souls
will never be able to wrap
their heads around the
pointless cruelty of others,
they weren't designed to.
-Kenzie D.

Sparkling lights and pine needles,
dusty ornaments and handmade stockings,
memories filled with choruses of endless laughter
strung together in the most beautiful series of songs.
Reminiscing on times filled with those we love
and the years we spent huddled around a deck of cards.
The smell of grandma's cooking that fills the
entire house with an aroma no one can replicate.
Years and years of happy tears,
that's what Christmas means to me.
-Kenzie D.

He treated her like a princess even though
her tiara was merely made of paper.
-Kenzie D.

Kenzie D.

I worked day and night to keep up
with the ever changing image you
expected me to portray,
the perfect picture frame I couldn't
seem to squeeze into. Like a bird with a
fractured wing still expected to fly,
I repeatedly jumped from the branch
innocently predicting to never hit the ground.
-Kenzie D.

Looking at the world full of hate and cruelty around her
she thought to herself that perhaps hell wasn't a place in
their nightmares, perhaps they were already there.
Although the world was ablaze,
she refused to believe it was beyond extinguishing.
-Kenzie D.

Love is the urge to understand,

the need for another's happiness.

Love is not broken promises,

it is not pushing another down in the effort to look taller.

Love is thc complete, sometimes blinding,

acceptance of the flaws painted on another's forehead.

It is all consuming.

-Kenzie D.

You have the rest of your life
to find out who you want to be.
Don't waste your innocent youth
tied up in the materialistic world of
briefcases and broken dreams.
-Kenzie D.

Her life crumbled around her as she sat in the
rubble trying frantically to fit the fragments
back together if only to let the façade
stand for a moment more.
She tried to think of the exact time in which the
decaying began. It happened so slowly that
she didn't see the cracks in the foundation,
she didn't hear the vacant echoes down the
empty halls beckoning her to join them
in their void of nothingness.
-Kenzie D.

The sweet melody transported
her to the last place she had heard it.

Driving down back roads and dreaming
of how their futures would change the world,
they were just two girls against everyone else.

With each beat a tear slid down her cheek as
she was reminded of all the things left undone.

She could have never imagined back then how
short their time left together would have been,
like a fleeting sunset that failed to rise.
-Kenzie D.

I live for the moments I can't put into words.

-Kenzie D.

She left lipstick stains on his broken heart
as she kissed the scattered parts of who
he used to be. A walking disaster with
menacing red lips. Though they were
nowhere near the sea, he could hear
her sirens call from miles away
always drawing him back to her.
-Kenzie D.

Her urge to run away vanished once she
discovered an endless adventure in his eyes.

-Kenzie D.

She was broken before they met
but still he spent endless hours
apologizing for things he had
never done just to convince her
they weren't all the same.
He mended a heart he had never
Broken and dried tears he didn't evoke.
-Kenzie D.

We all have a story to tell,
some are just brave enough to
share theirs with the world.
-Kenzie D.

All her life she jumped without looking,

did without asking,

always giving it her all.

She never did anything halfway,

her overzealous passion wouldn't hear of it.

She either loved you with every

piece of her being or not at all.

-Kenzie D.

Your drunken kisses taste like sober lies.

-Kenzie D.

A nightmare slowly emerged
from the dream she thought
she was living. So slowly
in fact that she didn't
realize it until she caught
herself making excuses for
each fragment of her
shattered heart, rationalizing
for the monster she fell in love with.
-Kenzie D.

Creativity is merely madness in the eyes of those
who see the world only as it is,
not as it could be.
-Kenzie D.

And she felt so indescribably,
blissfully happy.

The sun soaked into her skin,
energizing the optimist inside her.
Bringing light to pieces of herself
she had long forgotten.

The hopeful, innocent girl full of
dreams and passion was still a part of her.

She just needed a break from
self-doubt to discover her again.
-Kenzie D.

Can you hear us?

As we share memories of Christmas past and speak
your name.

Can you feel us?

As we radiate love and wishful thinking that Santa
would bring us you.

Merry Christmas wherever you are…

-Kenzie D.

Through it all, the heartache and the sorrow,
there was never a point when I was
willing to accept that that was the
way life was supposed to be.
No, there were greater things on the
horizon than anything that lay
rotting in the shadows.
-Kenzie D.

The chill that filled the air was nothing in comparison to the chill that racked her bones when she heard your name.

-Kenzie D.

Minute by minute the hands ticked by,
ever so quickly nearing the looming twelve.
As she reflected over the year,
she was met with both happiness and regret.
Closing her eyes she made a silent
promise to live this year for herself,
to put her needs and dreams in the
forefront of her mind.
-Kenzie D.

The black spider slowly crept onto the
palm of her open hand.
She smiled as she watched it run.
She embraced the things that once scared her,
for nothing could be as terrifying as who she had become.
-Kenzie D.

She wished her life was a movie where
even the worst of times are accompanied
by a beautiful melancholy soundtrack.
-Kenzie D.

His heart called to mine so strongly
that I heard it through my dreams
before I even knew whose voice it was.
I spent endless hours searching the
earth for the piece of my soul that
I knew was waiting for me inside you.
-Kenzie D.

As the waves kiss the horizon every day,
As the sun ceases to shine in lieu of the moon,
I will always find myself falling in love with you,
Day after day.
-Kenzie D.

Just because it is in the past does not mean
my heart no longer bleeds for the cause.
-Kenzie D.

She adorns herself with flaws
for she fears if someone loves
her they will only be infatuated
by the presentable fragments
of her broken persona.
In the fear of disapproval
she pushed anyone who showed
interest in her away,
never believing that a soul so
flawed could be worth loving.
-Kenzie D.

What an overwhelming sensation it is to
finally realize you are enough after
years of struggling to find your self-worth.
-Kenzie D.

The rain danced on the pavement to the
melancholy chorus of thunder,
cleansing the world with each drop.
For you must overcome the
clouds to be touched by the sun.
-Kenzie D.

And there it was,

happily ever after staring her in the face

and yet she still wasn't sure she knew

how to write the rest of her story.

Her hand shook each time the pen

neared the paper in fear of

past mistakes she could never erase.

-Kenzie D.

Her mind held the depths of the oceans,
the waves slowly eroding her thoughts.
She knew one day she would be swept out to the horizon.
There would be a day she would no longer be
strong enough to swim against the currents and
no life saver that he threw her would be
enough to pull her back to him.
-Kenzie D.

I cannot be held responsible for what my pen whispers in the glow of lamplight on a lonely night.
-Kenzie D.

You were a winter storm that
unpredictably took over her life,
a wind that whipped around her
turning her in every direction.
Leaving her frantically searching for shelter.
She fell into a sleepy trance,
hypnotized by your beauty,
and laid her head on the fresh powder.
So overwhelmed by the wonders
of you that she would
freeze to death before
ever giving up on loving you.
-Kenzie D.

Sometimes I feel so distant from you and it terrifies me, as if I've lost you all over again. But out here…

Out here I feel you everywhere.
-Kenzie D.

When you begin commenting on the parts of her
appearance that don't meet your unrealistic
standards you are showing the world
that you are ignorant enough to overlook
all the things that make her worth loving.
-Kenzie D.

She stood amongst the pines and
realized how small she truly was in this world.
With each breath of pure frigid air she could
feel her worries becoming less significant in her mind,
floating off between the mountains
and melting with the snow.
-Kenzie D.

She fell in love with the idea of how things could be,
the idea of how things were expected to be,
the thought of someone loving her,
the thought that she could someday love herself.

But like a miserable drunk finds comfort in the
bottle time and time again,
she chose not to see the ever present signs,
not to see the way the world was turning
while she was too busy standing still,
she chose to blindly love a man who did
so little to make it worth all her sacrifices.
-Kenzie D.

Blue is the world around her.
Slowly seeping into her soul,
replacing the prisms of light that
once shown from within her.
-Kenzie D.

His lips were whiskey and she was parched.

-Kenzie D.

She was ignorant to how extraordinary she was,
but he saw the mountains move in her presence.
A force to be reckoned with,
yet she was unaware of the strength
she carried in silent dignity through it all.
-Kenzie D.

The waves of the world
crashed down on her,
slamming her body
on the rocks that
lie on the ever eroding shore.
With each wave she began
to fight less and less.
The horizon began to
look dimmer as the
tide rose around her neck.
Currents pulled at her limp feet
and she finally let go,
allowing it to consume her.
She was overwhelmed with peace as
she drifted into the sunset.
-Kenzie D.

You don't have to like them,
you don't have to like what they do,
but you sure as hell better respect them.
-Kenzie D.

Write for the fragments of your
soul that beg to be heard.
-Kenzie D.

Let the wanderlust sink in.

The road is long and our spirits are free.

Oh darling, let's run away.

-Kenzie D.

Nothing could ever make you question everything
you have ever believed to be true
like the dissolution of someone you love.
-Kenzie D.

As they drove in the direction of reality
she realized that their adventure wasn't over.
As long as they had each other they would
explore the ends of the earth with
every momcnt they spent together.
-Kenzie D.

And there she was stuck between being
satisfied and being terrified…
-Kenzie D.

Wheat fields surrounding her,
the ground was soft beneath her
bare feet as she ran between
corn stalks laughing all the while.
Such child-like wonder
coursing through her veins,
every piece of her believed in a
future full of happiness and sunshine.
-Kenzie D.

The demons from within her
spilled through ink onto her paper as poetry.
-Kenzie D.

There were days that she was
crippled by unrealistic fears.
It came in crushing waves,
as if depression was the moon
that pulled the tides in over her.
Currents wrapped around her while
she fought fearfully to be free.
As the tears and salt water mixed
upon her cheeks, it was all she could
do to float rather than drown.
-Kenzie D.

Her soul itched for an escape,
for a new adventure,
but her mind held her feet planted in reality.
A never ending internal battle between doing
what she wants and doing what is expected.
-Kenzie D.

She prayed for a day when she wouldn't
cringe while looking into the mirror.
-Kenzie D.

The mountains are a beacon through the night,
guiding me down a single lane highway
as dusk kisses the horizon.
They call to the caged fragments of my soul,
begging me to set them free.
-Kenzie D.

It's riveting to know the freedom
you seek is supported by the one you love.
-Kenzie D.

It's something you could never explain
and even if you could,
they would never understand.
-Kenzie D.

She was mesmerized by the oceans inside his eyes,
hypnotized by the maps carved on his palms.
She knew he would take her places
she could never go alone,
to depths of emotions no other had ever evoked.
She vowed to spend the rest of her life
exploring what lies inside his mind.
-Kenzie D.

There are days when the sun seems to shine brighter,
the birds' songs seem to be in tune with your steps
and the air gives a fresh breath to the impurities
gathering dust in the depths of your insecurities.
-Kenzie D.

It wasn't you that I had a hard time letting go of,
it was the façade of the life I thought we had
that I couldn't pry from my grasp.
-Kenzie D.

If the world were to offer you a second chance,
would you take it?
Would you say all the things you never said?
Kiss the one you've always missed?
Would you watch the sunset one more
time with the one you love?
How many things would you take the chance to never say?
If the world were to give you a second chance,
would you leave behind the regrets of your future?
-Kenzie D.

I write so others can catch a glimpse
of the way I see the world.
I write with optimism that
my words will inspire others.
I write in the hopes of evoking emotions.
-Kenzie D.

Bottle caps and broken promises were
scattered around the floor like remnants
of the life we once shared.
-Kenzie D.

"Run away with me" sat so heavy on her tongue
that she knew she must say it before it rolled
off of its own will. Yet she was so scared of change,
so terrified of risk that she feared she may choke on the
words before releasing them to the world.
-Kenzie D.

No matter how many spirits she consumed
she knew it would never take the place
of the one missing from within her.
-Kenzie D.

Kenzie D.

Bliss spread through her like water through sand.
Overcoming misunderstood resistance
she eventually allowed it to soak her soul,
to cleanse her of the filth from the life she once led.
-Kenzie D.

My mind is full of tumble weeds
caught in tornadoes,

Fields of lilac during a
spring lightning storm,

A beautiful beach with fire
dancing upon the waves,

The morning sunrise as it is
overcome with a rolling fog,

Thinking of everything and
yet nothing at all.
-Kenzie D.

The lights glistened above them,
setting a scene from a movie.
She saw the skyline in his eyes
and it felt like home.
-Kenzie D.

Some days I dare not open my mouth in fear
that the pressures of the world would fall
from my tongue so easily I would be unable to stop them.

Sliding through my teeth,
each syllable a nail in the coffin of my strong façade
I have spent so many meticulous minutes building.
-Kenzie D.

Be the hero the universe forgot to send you.
-Kenzie D.

Do you understand the tortures
words can have on the mind?
The loss of love, the loss of life?
Negative words are hammers that slowly pound
in the nails of a coffin.
With each syllable one's
self esteem can visibly vanish.

Positive affirmations are sunrises that
awaken the optimist within you.
Shedding light on all the parts
of you that are worth loving.
-Kenzie D.

I'm overwhelmingly enthralled with passion
for so many arts that individually they
tend to not get pursued to their fullest potential.
-Kenzie D.

When you think you've done enough,
do a little bit more.

When you think you've been kind enough,
share one last smile.

When you think you've loved enough,
give out your heart one last time.

When you think you can do no more,
try just once more.
-Kenzie D.

It's funny how the world changes you.
How slowly your priorities change and
before you know it you are standing upside
down seeing the world from a skewed
perspective without realizing it.
-Kenzie D.

She wore rose colored glasses
that often fogged her vision.
-Kenzie D.

She always had a compulsive need to say she was sorry,
to apologize for the person she had become.
For never being the most educated,
for never being the most well-spoken,
for having opinions that differed from others,
for needing to be loved as fiercely as she loved,
for never being as strong as she thought she should be,
for rambling when passion ran through her,
for showing weakness in the presence of indifference,
for never being what someone expected,
for never being what someone needed,
for never being enough.
-Kenzie D.

Tomorrow is an elusive lottery ticket
that many never get to cash.
-Kenzie D.

She clung to a hope that had long been lost.
So exhaustingly gripping at the strands of a
past long gone that effortlessly slipped through
her eager fingers that she allowed herself to
forget why she made it a part of her past so many years
ago.
-Kenzie D.

You mustn't seek happiness in
the source of your pain.
Although you will it with
all your might to be so,
you will never find light at
the end of a crumbled tunnel.
-Kenzie D.

Maybe somewhere in another universe
they would have been made for one another.
Maybe in another life they could have continued
forward when their paths met.
Maybe at another time they could have
made the clocks stand still for them.
Maybe, just maybe.
-Kenzie D.

Don't allow yourself to become
comfortable in the void that lies
between past mistakes and futuristic fears.
-Kenzie D.

Lying in bed she prayed for the world to change,
for happiness to overcome her even if unprovoked,
for war to end and peace to fill the hearts of all,
for hunger to be something no child
ever has to understand, she prayed for a world
she knew she would never live to see.
-Kenzie D.

Break a writer's heart and you will live
infinitely on the crumpled pages of an old
tear stained notebook that rots on a shelf
at the back of her closet, begging to be forgiven.
-Kenzie D.

Hold me tight as the sky holds the sun,
wrapping it in warmth with the
promise to always cradle it,
never allowing it to fall.

Envelop me in love as the stars shield the moon,
always shining in his presence,
promising to be a beacon in the night
when he eclipses into himself.
-Kenzie D.

You showed me what true love was,
how I should have been treated all along.
-Kenzie D.

Am I the only one who feels things this deeply?
The only one who cries for lives of those I've never met?
Who tears up each time the national anthem is played?
Or a puppy finds a new home?
Am I the only one who finds a quiet backroad at
sunset heart-wrenchingly beautiful?
-Kenzie D.

She begged for a storm to roll in,

anything to attribute her sadness to.

She felt maddened by her swift emotional changes,

unaware of the cause of them.

Silently she prayed for lightening to fill the room,

for any reason at all to feel so uneasy.

-Kenzie D.

It isn't until I don't know where else to
turn that I fall to my knees,
not until I desperately seek you that I begin to look.
I laid at her bedside and begged you to make her better,
I pleaded to hear her voice one more time,
to share a few moments more filled with laughter.
I begged, I pleaded, I cried to no avail.
-Kenzie D.

It has always been you.
Even years before I knew
your face or the sound of your voice,
I could feel my love for you growing day by day.
-Kenzie D.

I sit before an empty desk that houses
merely one lonely notebook staring blankly
at the pages as they return the favor.
With a pen burning into my palm,
not allowing me to forget it's presence,
I struggle with whether or not
I have a story worth telling.
Fleeting words in my mind taunt me as they
float to the abyss before I am able to collect them,
never to be seen again.
-Kenzie D.

What is love if not a continual rush of
falling from a cliff with no end in sight?
It is but a strenuous adventure with a
guide more persistent than any other.
A ship whose captain's destination could
be recharted at the slightest change of wind,
sending him on an exploration unlike any other.
-Kenzie D.

Write your story on my lips.

Each kiss a revelation of your true self.

Express yourself the only way you know how,

with each beat of your pounding heart

unraveling the facade you want the world to see.

-Kenzie D.

She wears her scars like war paint,
each mark a reminder of a past she can never forget.
For every visible scar there are infinite
more that are out of sight,
they rest heavily on her soul and carry a weight
on her heart that is slowly cracking in the wake
of the insecurities he created within her.
-Kenzie D.

Wine is the spark that turns
madness into creativity,
it sets fire to the parts of
you that have been begging to be heard,
your heart is caught ablaze and your
whole facade reduces to embers around you.
-Kenzie D.

For the first time in her life she did what
she wanted without concern for others.
She leapt from the mound of self-doubt and
uncertainty that had slowly built around her
with the hopes of growing wings on the way down.
-Kenzie D.

What are we in comparison to the
stars that shine above us?
Merely a speck of energy among an infinite
galaxy of undiscovered wonder?
-Kenzie D.

Your laugh will always call me to you,
despite the roars of the world around me,
I will hear the joy in your voice,
and I will find you yet again.

Your smile will always light my way home,
regardless of the darkness that
threatens to engulf me,
the pure bliss of your lips will pull me to you.

You will always be my center of gravity,
even in the times I feel my world is
spinning from orbit with a mix of
confusion and despair.
-Kenzie D.

Here in this moment,
with my feet on your lap and
a glass of wine in my hand,
I feel at home.
-Kenzie D.

Despite the frigid air surrounding her,
she was filled with warmth at the
thought of their time together.
As the raindrops mixed with tears
that streamed down her cheeks,
she dropped the single white rose
onto the unturned ground.
-Kenzie D.

Headlights shining on the road before us,
illuminating the lane,
looking over at you,
my worries began to melt away.
With the music up,
and dust flying all around,
getting lost with you on a backroad,
feels a lot like being found.
-Kenzie D.

She didn't know what her dreams consisted of
but she knew they were bigger
than her world had to offer.
-Kenzie D.

Green were his eyes as they danced under the stars,
a bottle of whiskey in hand.
Twirling together to the music,
she knew she had never been so lucky.
-Kenzie D.

A hero gone too young.
As the moon sacrifices himself so the sun can shine,
you sacrificed your life for our freedom.
My heart both cherishes and weeps for you.
May your soul rest peacefully under the
red and blue that wave pridefully above you.
You have left footprints on our soil and handprints on
our flag.
-Kenzie D.

Air rushing through my hair I stood in
my seat with my head out the roof and
yelled into the wind. My God did I feel free.

-Kenzie D.

He created insecurities and self-doubt
within you that you didn't deserve.
He fed on your anxiety and mocked
your depression, as if it wasn't an emotion
you were allowed to feel.
And yet still you justified his actions,
making excuses for him until you
were blue in the face.

It's hard to make a victim out of a villain.
-Kenzie D.

My mind is a broken record as it skips over the
shattered fragments only remembering to
play a beautiful tune time and time again.
-Kenzie D.

A curious thing it is when one can find what
they need inside the words of another.

-Kenzie D.

Is it possible to truly begin again?
Or does your past follow you around
like a dark looming shadow threatening to
catch your feet with each step towards your future?
-Kenzie D.

I have a way of spinning pain into beautiful
sentences structured by secrets and
strung together with insecurities.
-Kenzie D.

The waves tumbled over her,

pulling her head under for longer amounts of time,

eventually submerging her entirely.

It took over her slowly, wave by wave

until she no longer had the strength to fight.

Over the white caps she could see him in the distance,

fighting the current with all his might.

A tear slid down her cheek as she watched his struggle,

wishing he would give up on her.

She was afraid he couldn't pull her back to shore this time,

maybe she was no longer worth saving.

-Kenzie D.

Flames licked the sky as they sipped from mason jars.
Laughter filled the air around them,
never had she been so unapologetically happy.
-Kenzie D.

How can I quiet my mind?
My soul is at peace and yet my
mind is screaming for things beyond my control.
What will it take to make it stop?
To silence the anxieties who refuse to go unheard?
-Kenzie D.

She was made of stardust and constellations,
every thought a shooting star intended for wishing.
The moon was dim in comparison to the galaxies that
rested in the glimmer of her eyes.

-Kenzie D.

If I knew what I know now when it all began,

I would go back to that night and save

myself the heartache of loving a shell

who was incapable of loving me in return.

I would remind myself that I was

worth so much more than you were able to offer.

-Kenzie D.

She screamed out loud in the hopes
that the wind would carry away all the
things she never dared to say,
all the hate that ate at her once pure soul.
-Kenzie D.

Writing cleanses the soul,
clears the pallet
and heightens your senses.
-Kenzie D.

She clung to a hope that had long been lost.
An idea that she knew would never be,
as you cannot return sand to an hourglass,
she knew they could never be who they once were.
So much had changed between them that
she knew despite her endless efforts they
could never turn back time.
-Kenzie D.

Although she often awoke with
reasons to be bitter on her mind,
she chose to be happy day after day

and that is important.
-Kenzie D.

She was like sand.
Seeming so solid in appearance
but slipping through his fingers when
they were in the absence of others,
turning to an unrecognizable mess at his feet.
-Kenzie D.

The words sounded like Merlot
pouring off his tongue,
leaving her wanting nothing more
than to drink them up.
-Kenzie D.

She realized that overlooking all of his faults
to focus on his few good qualities was
like searching an endless beach seeking
a diamond in the sand, tiring and
ultimately not worth all the wasted energy.
-Kenzie D.

Surrounded by friendly faces,
she had never felt more alone.
Silently she begged for someone,
anyone, to notice her.
-Kenzie D.

The waves kissed her toes
and nervously pulled away
before she was given a chance
to appreciate their gentle nature.
They retreated to the horizon time
and time again as the fleeting sun
gave a sense of optimism for the
days yet to come.
-Kenzie D.

A heart can still feel pain in the absence of love.
Removing the cause of sadness in your life
doesn't magically mend a broken heart.
-Kenzie D.

Take me back to under the mulberry tree
where we laughed all day and
made memories we could never forget.
-Kenzie D.

After it crashing down,
her world finally began to slowly spin again.
She wished now only to convince herself
it was spinning in the correct direction.
-Kenzie D.

Nothing will torture your mind quite like
the nightmares of past memories you want
to forget replaying night after night,
interrupting your restless slumber.
-Kenzie D.

Pushing the petal flat to the floor
she laughed in the face of adrenaline.
If it was such a rush to live,
she imagined what a rush it would be to die.
-Kenzie D.

Why is it that the gentle souls end up
breaking their backs to carry the burdens
of those who would never lend a helping hand
when the load became too heavy to bear?
-Kenzie D.

I'm so oblivious to my life before him.
To the way I used to feel,
the innocent and carefree way I
used to view my world.
I no longer know who I am,
no longer know how to be happy.
I don't know if I like myself
in the absence of pain.
-Kenzie D.

My life has moved forward,

leaps and bounds I have conquered my past.

Although I no longer pine for things long gone,

my heart still bleeds at the thought of the pain it evoked.

-Kenzie D.

You believe too heavily in my
strength for either of our own goods…
-Kenzie D.

He was a hawk and I merely a field
mouse unable to defend myself against his grasp.
-Kenzie D.

There is a rolling meadow
that lies between
certainty and hesitation.
Darling, meet me there.
-Kenzie D.

Whether it be comforting a
friend or hugging a stranger,
do what you can to reach out to those around you.
For we are all only stumbling through life
together and it is much easier to find the strength
to continue when you have a hand to hold.
-Kenzie D.

About the Author

Kenzie D. currently lives in a small town in Oklahoma with her dog, Aspen.

She has been passionate about writing for as long as she can remember. Now that she has delved back into it, she couldn't be happier. Kenzie values her family above all else; without them, she would never have had the drive to publish her first book, *Words*.

She is currently writing her first full-length novel and looks forward to publishing more books in the future.

20728754R00125

Printed in Great Britain
by Amazon